Merry

Orlin !

Christmas 1978

— Jan, Art, Amy, John

A House Divided

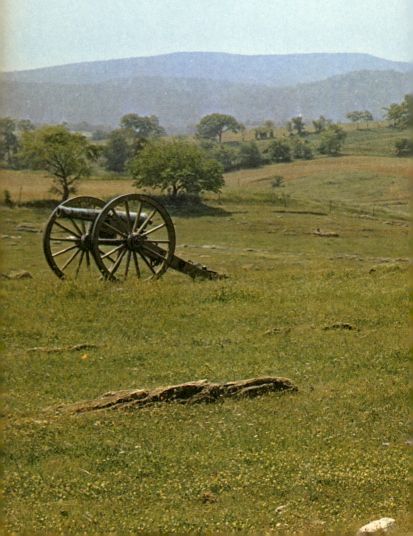

A HOUSE

*Illustrated with Photographs
of the Major Battlegrounds*

DIVIDED

A Treasury

of the Civil War

Hallmark Editions

Edited by David Stark and Peter Seymour
Photographs by Richard L. Gunn
and David E. Scherman

CONTENTS

A HOUSE DIVIDED

» All One Thing, or All the Other «

On June 16, 1858, in Springfield, Illinois, Abraham Lincoln accepted the Republican nomination for United States Senator. His acceptance speech drove to the heart of the growing conflict:

If we could first know where we are, and whither we are tending, we could then better judge what to do, and how to do it. We are now in the fifth year since a policy was initiated with the avowed object and confident promise of putting an end to slavery agitation. Under the operation of that policy, that agitation has not only not ceased, but has constantly augmented. In my opinion, it will not cease, until a crisis shall have been reached and passed—"A house divided against itself cannot stand." I believe this government cannot endure, permanently half slave and half free. I do not expect the Union to be dissolved—I do not expect the house to fall—but I do expect it will cease to be divided. It will become all one thing, or all the other. Either the opponents of slavery will arrest the further spread of it, and place it where the public mind shall rest in the belief that it is in course of ultimate extinction; or its advocates will push it forward till it shall become alike lawful in all the States, old as well as new—North as well as South.

John Brown's Last Speech

Found guilty of murder and of conspiring with slaves and others to rebel, fiery abolitionist John Brown was asked why a sentence of death should not be passed upon him. His reply, on November 2, 1859, states his case against slavery:

I have, may it please the court, a few words to say. In the first place, I deny everything but what I have all along admitted—the design on my part to free the slaves. . . . I never did intend murder, or treason, or the destruction of property, or to excite or incite slaves to rebellion, or to make insurrection. . . . It is unjust that I should suffer such a penalty. Had I interfered in the manner which I admit, and which I admit has been fairly proved . . . had I so interfered in behalf of the rich, the powerful, the intelligent, the so-called great, or in behalf of any of their friends . . . and suffered and sacrificed what I have in this interference, it would have been all right; and every man in this court would have deemed it an act worthy of reward rather than punishment.

This court acknowledges, as I suppose, the validity of the law of God. I see a book kissed here which I suppose to be the Bible, or at least the New Testament. That teaches me that all things whatsoever I would that men should do to me, I should do even so to them. It teaches me, further, to "remember them that are in bonds, as bound with them." I endeavored to act up to that instruction. I say, I am yet too young to understand that God is any respecter of persons. I believe that to have interfered as I have done—as I have always freely admitted I have done—in behalf of His despised poor, was not wrong, but right. Now it is deemed necessary that I should forfeit my life for the furtherance of the ends of justice, and mingle my blood further with the blood of my children and with the blood of millions in this slave country whose rights are disregarded by wicked, cruel, and unjust enactments—I submit; so let it be done!

Secession

The first state formally to declare its secession from the Union was South Carolina, on December 20, 1860:

We, the people of the State of South Carolina, in Convention assembled, do declare and ordain, and it is hereby declared and ordained, that the ordinance adopted by us in Convention, on the 23rd day of May, in the year of our Lord 1788, whereby the Constitution of the United States of America was ratified, and also all Acts and parts of Acts of the General Assembly of this State ratifying the amendments of the said Constitution, are hereby repealed, and that the union now subsisting between South Carolina and other States under the name of the United States of America is hereby dissolved.

Robert E. Lee Resigns

When North and South split, and war was at hand, many men faced the heartache of divided loyalties. Robert E. Lee, perhaps the most distinguished officer in the United States Army, chose home above country. He wrote to General Winfield Scott, his superior officer, of his decision:

Arlington, Virginia, April 20, 1861
General Scott: Since my interview with you on the 18th inst. I have felt that I ought no longer to retain my commission in the Army. I therefore tender my resignation, which I request you will recommend for acceptance. It would have been presented at once but for the struggle it has cost me to separate myself from a service to which I have devoted the best years of my life, and all the ability I possessed. During the whole of that time—more than a quarter of a century—I have experienced nothing but kindness from my superiors and a most cordial friendship from my comrades. To no one, General, have I been as much indebted as to yourself for uniform kindness and consideration, and it has always been my ardent desire to merit your approbation. I shall carry to the grave the most grateful recollections of your kind consideration, and your name and fame shall always be dear

to me. Save in defense of my native State, I never desire again to draw my sword.

Be pleased to accept my most earnest wishes for the continuance of your happiness and prosperity, and believe me most truly yours,

R. E. Lee

Lee also wrote, apologetically, to his sister in the North:

Arlington, Virginia, April 20, 1861

My Dear Sister: I am grieved at my inability to see you. . . . I have been waiting for a "more convenient season," which has brought to many before me deep and lasting regret. Now we are in a state of war which will yield to nothing. The whole South is in a state of revolution, into which Virginia, after a long struggle, has been drawn; and though I recognize no necessity for this state of things, and would have forborne and pleaded to the end for redress of grievances, real or supposed, yet in my own person I had to meet the question whether I should take part against my native State.

With all my devotion to the Union and the feeling of loyalty and duty of an American citizen, I have not been able to make up my mind to raise my hand against my relatives, my children, my home. I have therefore resigned my commission in the Army, and save in defense of my native State, with the sincere hope that my poor services may never be needed, I hope I may never be called on to draw my sword. I know you will blame me; but you must think as kindly of me as you can, and believe that I have endeavoured to do what I thought right.

To show you the feeling and struggle it has cost me, I send you a copy of my letter of resignation. I have no time for more. May God guard and protect you and yours, and shower upon you everlasting blessings, is the prayer of your devoted brother,

R. E. Lee

BATTLE IS JOINED

The First Shots

The first shots of the Civil War were fired on a small Union garrison at Fort Sumter, which sat in the harbor of Confederate-controlled Charleston. Mary Chestnut, whose husband participated in the Confederate bombardment, records the event in her diary:

I do not pretend to go to sleep. How can I? If Anderson does not accept terms at four [a.m.] the orders are he shall be fired upon. I count four, St. Michael's bells chime out, and I begin to hope. At half past four the heavy booming of a cannon. I sprang out of bed, and on my knees prostrate I prayed as I never prayed before. There was a sound of stir all over the house, pattering of feet in the corridors. All seemed hurrying one way. I put on my double gown and a shawl and went too. It was to the housetop. The shells were bursting. . . . The regular roar of the cannon, there it was. And who could tell what each volley accomplished of death and destruction?

The women were wild there on the housetop.

Prayers came from the women and imprecations from the men. And then a shell would light up the scene. Tonight they say the forces are to attempt to land. We watched up there, and everybody wondered that Fort Sumter did not fire a shot. . . .

We hear nothing, can listen to nothing; boom, boom, goes the cannon all the time. The nervous strain is awful, alone in this darkened room. "Richmond and Washington ablaze," say the papers—blazing with excitement. Why not? To us these last days' events seem frightfully great. We were all women on that iron balcony. Men are only seen at a distance now.

Major Robert Anderson, commander of Fort Sumter, reports its surrender:

Steamship Baltic, off Sandy Hook,
April 18, 1861, 10:30 A.M.

Hon. S. Cameron, Secretary of War,
Washington, D.C.
Sir: Having defended Fort Sumter for thirty-four hours, until the quarters were entirely burned, the main gates destroyed by fire, the gorge wall seriously injured, the magazine surrounded by flames, and its door closed from the effect of the heat, four barrels and three cartridges of powder only being available, and no provisions but pork remaining, I accepted terms of evacuation, offered by General Beauregard, being the same offered by him on the 11th inst., prior

to the commencement of hostilities, and marched out of the fort Sunday afternoon, the 14th inst., with colors flying and drums beating, bringing away company and private property, and saluting my flag with fifty guns.

Robert Anderson, Major, First Artillery

Call for Troops

No one expected a long war. No one expected half a million deaths. Men young and old rushed into uniform—toward a great adventure. Poet and historian Carl Sandburg describes the Southern armies:

Among troops at Richmond were farmers and hill-men who never owned a slave nor an acre of ground, and young men from the First Families where a thousand acres and a hundred slaves was the unit. Dapper companies with shining blouses, brass buttons, uniform rifles of recent make, were regimented with other companies in butternut jeans, carrying shotguns and squirrel rifles.

From the Potomac River to the Gulf Coast and out where the Rio Grande trickled over New Mexico ran the recruiting ground of this Confederate Army. Its line zigzagged 1,500 miles from Chesapeake Bay through Kentucky and out to the corners of Kansas. Its brain and will centered in the capitol, the executive mansion, the departments, at Richmond. Its chief weapon of defense was an army of 100,000 troops.

President Lincoln's message to Congress on July 4, 1861, rallies the North:

It is now recommended that you give the legal means for making this contest a short and decisive one: that you place at the control of the government, for the work, at least four hundred thousand men and $400,-000,000. That number of men is about one-tenth of those of proper ages within the regions where, apparently, *all* are willing to engage; and the sum is less than a twenty-third part of the money value owned by the men who seem ready to devote the whole. A debt of $600,000,000 *now*, is a less sum per head, than was the debt of our Revolution, when we came out of that struggle; and the money value in the country now bears even a greater proportion to what it was *then*, than does the population. Surely each man has as strong a motive *now*, to preserve our liberties, as each had *then*, to *establish* them.

The First Battle of Bull Run

Here the war became reality at last. Historian Bruce Catton reconstructs the event:

There is nothing in American military history quite like the story of Bull Run. It was the momentous fight of the amateurs, the battle where everything went wrong, the great day of awakening for the whole nation, North and South together. It marked the end of the ninety-day militia, and it also ended the rosy time in which men could dream that the war would be short, glorious, and bloodless. After Bull Run the nation got down to business. . . .

The Rebel army at Bull Run was in no better shape than the Federal army, but when the showdown came it was able to fight on the defensive—which, as numerous battles in this war would show, was infinitely easier for untrained troops. . . . A good many men ran away, to be sure, but most of them stayed and fought, and the struggle was a hot one. For a time it seemed that the Confederate line would be broken and that the "Forward to Richmond" motif would come to a triumphant crescendo. The two regular batteries that had been doing such good work were advanced to the crest of Henry House Hill, infantry came surging along with them, and a number of the Confederate units weakened and began to drift to the rear.

Then came one of those moments of dramatic inspiration that men remember. Brigadier General Barnard Bee sought to rally some of the wavering Confederate regiments. Not far away he saw a Virginia brigade of Johnston's troops, standing fast and delivering a sharp fire: a brigade led by that former V.M.I. professor, Brigadier General T. J. Jackson.

"There is Jackson standing like a stone wall!" cried Bee, gesturing with his sword. "Rally behind the Virginians!"

So a great name was born. From that moment on the man would be Stonewall Jackson.

'Most of them stayed and fought. . . .'

Bee's troops rallied. Fresh Confederate troops, just off the train from the Valley, kept coming in on their flank. The two pestiferous Union batteries, placed too far forward to get proper support from their own infantry, were taken by a sudden Confederate counterattack—the Rebels here wore blue uniforms, and the gunners held their fire until too late, supposing the attacking wave to be Unionists coming up to help —and suddenly the Union offensive, which had come so near to success, collapsed, all the heart gone out of it, and the soldiers who had been involved in it turned and headed for the rear.

There was no rout here. The Union attack had failed and the men were withdrawing, but there was no panic. One trouble apparently lay in the fact that the tactical maneuver by which troops fighting in line would form column and go to the rear was very complicated, and most of these green Union troops did not have it down pat; a withdrawal under fire was bound to become disordered and finally uncontrollable, not because the men had lost their courage but simply because they had not had enough drill. McDowell saw that nothing more could be done here and passed the word for a retreat to his advance base at Centerville, four or five miles nearer Washington.

It was after the beaten army had crossed Bull Run that the real trouble came, and the fault lies less with the soldiers than with the reckless Washington civilians who had supposed that the edge of a battlefield would be an ideal place for a picnic.

A civilian eye-witness, W. W. Blackford, describes the climax at Bull Run:
But now the most extraordinary spectacle I have ever witnessed took place. I had been gazing at the numerous well-formed lines as they moved forward to the attack, some fifteen or twenty thousand strong in full view, and for some reason had turned my head in another direction for a moment, when some one exclaimed, pointing to the battlefield, "Look! Look!"

I looked, and what a change had taken place in an instant. Where those "well-dressed," well-defined lines, with clear spaces between, had been steadily pressing forward, the whole field was a confused swarm of men, like bees, running away as fast as their legs could carry them, with all order and organ- ization abandoned. In a moment more the whole val- ley was filled with them as far as the eye could reach. They plunged through Bull Run wherever they came to it regardless of fords or bridges, and there many were drowned. Muskets, cartridge boxes, belts, knap- sacks, haversacks and blankets were thrown away in their mad race, that nothing might impede their flight. In the reckless haste the artillery drove over everyone who did not get out of their way. Ambu- lance and wagon drivers cut the traces and dashed off on the mules. . . .

Numbers of gay members of Congress had come

out from Washington to witness the battle from the adjacent hills, provided with baskets of champagne and lunches. So there was a regular chariot race when the rout began. We found, occasionally, along the road, parasols and dainty shawls lost in their flight by the frail, fair ones who had seats in most of the carriages of this excursion.

Monitor *Vs.* Merrimack

Naval engagements played only secondary roles in the war, but one of them was the historic battle between the first ironclads in March, 1862. Confederate Commander R. E. Colston tells what he saw:

For an instant they seemed to pause, as if to survey each other. Then advancing cautiously, the two vessels opened fire as soon as they came within range, and a fierce artillery duel raged between them without preceptible effect, although the entire fight was within close range, from a half mile at the farthest down to a few yards. For four hours, from 8 to 12 (which seemed three times as long), the cannonading continued with hardly a moment's intermission. I was now within three-quarters of a mile of them, and more than once stray shots came near enough to dash the spray over my barge, but the grandeur of the spectacle was so fascinating that they passed by unheeded. During the evolutions, in which the *Monitor* had the advantage of light draught, the *Merrimack* ran aground. After much delay and difficulty she was floated off. Finding that her shot made no impression whatever upon the *Monitor*, the *Merrimack*, seizing a favorable chance, succeeded in striking her foe with her stem. Soon afterward they ceased firing and separated as if by common consent. The *Monitor* steamed away toward Old Point. . . . The *Merrimack* steamed slowly toward Norfolk, evidently disabled in her motive power.

Thoughts Before Battle

A young Union seaman speaks for all his compatriots in this moving excerpt from a letter home:

How strange, peculiar, and indescribable are one's feelings when going into battle. There is a light-heartedness—a quickening of all the springs of life. There is thrill in every nerve—an exhilaration of spirit—a tension of every fibre. You see every movement, hear every sound, and think not only of what is before you, but of home, of the loved ones there— of the possibility that you may never behold them again. Some men review their lives, and ask themselves if they have left anything undone which ought to have been done—if their lives have been complete.

ON THE FRONT LINES

Confusion at the Rear

Soldiers and others with first-hand battle experience seldom glamorize war. They remember blood and death, fear and destruction, ironic accidents and the blunt grief of loss. But they recall courage too, and often the humor of war. Union General William T. Sherman remarks the disarray he found behind battle lines:

I never saw the rear of an army engaged in battle but I feared that some calamity had happened at the front—the apparent confusion, broken wagons, crippled horses, men lying about dead and maimed, parties hastening to and fro in seeming disorder, and a general apprehension of something dreadful about to ensue; all these signs, however, lessened as I neared the front, and there the contract was complete—perfect order, men and horses full of confidence, and it was not unusual for general hilarity, laughing, and cheering. Although cannon might be firing, the musketry clattering, and the enemy's shot hitting close, there reigned a general feeling of strength and security that bore a marked contrast to the bloody signs that had drifted rapidly to the rear; therefore, for comfort and safety, I surely would rather be at the front than the rear line of battle.

Dividing the Catch

An anonymous story reminds us of the inequality of rank, and the resentment it often produced:

A lad on a Union gunboat was kneeling in prayer just as the vessel was going into action, and an officer sneeringly asked him if he was afraid.

"No, I was praying," was the response.

"Well, what were you praying for?" asked the officer.

"Praying that the enemy's bullets may be distributed the same as the prize money is, principally among the officers."

Aerial Warfare

Balloons were used frequently in the war as elevated observation posts. Confederate General James Longstreet laments the loss of a particularly valuable balloon to the "Federals":

The Federals had been using balloons in examining our positions, and we watched with envious eyes their beautiful observations as they floated high up in the air, well out of range of our guns. While we were longing for the balloons that poverty denied us, a genius arose for the occasion and suggested that we send out and gather silk dresses in the Confederacy and make a balloon. It was done, and we soon had a great patchwork ship of many varied hues which was ready for use in the Seven Days' campaign.

We had no gas except in Richmond, and it was the custom to inflate the balloon there, tie it securely to an engine, and run it down the York River Railroad to any point at which we desired to send it up. One day it was on a steamer down on the James River, when the tide went out and left the vessel and balloon high and dry on a bar. The Federals gathered it in, and with it the last silk dress in the Confederacy. This capture was the meanest trick of the war and one that I have never yet forgiven.

Shiloh

This bloodiest battle of the war in the West inspired many poems. Herman Melville, author of Moby Dick, *wrote one of the best:*

Skimming lightly, wheeling still,
   The swallows fly low
Over the field in clouded days,
   The forest field of Shiloh—
Over the field where April rain
Solaced the parched one stretched in pain
Through the pause of night
That followed the Sunday fight
   Around the church of Shiloh—
The church so lone, the log-built one,

That echoed to many a parting groan
　　And natural prayer
　　Of dying foemen mingled there—
Foemen at morn, but friends at eve—
　　Fame or country least their care:
(What like a bullet can undeceive!)
　　But now they lie low,
While over them the swallows skim,
　　And all is hushed at Shiloh.

» The Red Badge of Courage «

In 1895, Stephen Crane, who had never seen a battle, published a brilliant and realistic novel, The Red Badge of Courage, *about the futility of war as seen through the eyes of a Union youth:*

This advance of the enemy had seemed to the youth like a ruthless hunting. He began to fume with rage and exasperation. He beat his foot upon the ground, and scowled with hate at the swirling smoke that was approaching like a phantom flood. There was a maddening quality in this seeming resolution of the foe to give him no rest, to give him no time to sit down and think. Yesterday he had fought and had fled rapidly. There had been many adventures. For to-day he felt that he had earned opportunities for contemplative repose. . . .

But those other men seemed never to grow weary; they were fighting with their old speed. He had a wild hate for the relentless foe. Yesterday, when he had imagined the universe to be against him, he had hated it, little gods and big gods; to-day he hated the army of the foe with the same great hatred. He was not going to be badgered of his life, like a kitten chased by boys, he said. It was not well to drive men into final corners; at those moments they could all develop teeth and claws.

He leaned and spoke into his friend's ear. He menaced the woods with a gesture. "If they keep on chasing us, by Gawd, they'd better watch out. Can't stand *too* much."

The friend twisted his head and made a calm reply. "If they keep on a-chasin' us they'll drive us all inteh th' river."

The youth cried out savagely at this statement. . . . His fingers twined nervously about his rifle. He wished that it was an engine of annihilating power. He felt that he and his companions were being taunted and derided from sincere convictions that they were poor and puny. His knowledge of his inability to take vengeance for it made his rage into a dark and stormy specter, that possessed him and made him dream of abominable cruelties.

» Cavalry Crossing a Ford «

In a famous poem, Walt Whitman re-creates the picturesqueness of moving cavalry:

A line in long array where they wind betwixt
    green islands,

They take a serpentine course, their arms flash in
    the sun—hark to the musical clank,
Behold the silvery river, in it the splashing
    horses loitering stop to drink,
Behold the brown-faced men, each group, each person
    a picture, the negligent rest on the saddles,
Some emerge on the opposite bank, others are just
    entering the ford—while,
Scarlet and blue and snowy white,
The guidon flags flutter gayly in the wind.

Stonewall Jackson Dies

*At Jackson's side, the Reverend J. P. Powers recalls
the great Southern general's death in May, 1863:*
The long day was passed with bright hopes for the
wounded general, with tidings of success of the
battlefield, with sad news of losses, and messages to
and from other wounded officers brought to the same
infirmary.

On Monday, the general was carried in an ambu-
lance, by the way of Spotsylvania Court House, to
most comfortable lodging at Chandler's, near Guin-
ea's Station, on the Richmond, Federicksburg and
Potomac railroad. And here, against our hopes, not-
withstanding the skill and care of wise and watchful
surgeons, attended day and night by wife and friends,
amid the prayers and tears of all the Southern land,
thinking not of himself, but of the cause he loved,
and for the troops who had followed him so well and

'Amid the prayers . . . of all the Southern land. . . .'

given him so great a name, our chief sank, day by day, with symptoms of pneumonia and some pains of pleurisy, until, at 3:15 P.M. on the quiet Sabbath afternoon, May 10, 1863, he raised himself from his bed, saying, "No, no, let us cross over the river, and rest under the shade of the trees"; and, falling again to his pillow, he passed away, over the river, where, in a land where warfare is not known or feared, he rests forever "under the trees."

Northern Strength

Most Southern troops realized that the North had superior supplies and equipment. General William T. Sherman comments in his memoirs:

The rebel soldiers felt that it was a waste of labor for them to march hurriedly, on wide circuits, day and night, to burn a bridge and tear up a mile or so of track, when they knew that we could lay it back so quickly. They supposed that we had men and money without limit, and that we always kept on hand, distributed along the road, duplicates of every bridge and culvert of any importance.

According to one who was on Kenesaw Mountain during our advance in the previous June or July, a group of rebels lay in the shade of a tree, one hot day, overlooking our camps about Big Shanty.

One soldier remarked to his fellows:

"Well, the Yanks will have to git up and git now, for I heard General Johnston himself say that General Wheeler had blown up the tunnel near Dalton, and that the Yanks would have to retreat, because they could get no more rations."

"Oh, hell!" said a listener, "don't you know that old Sherman carries a duplicate tunnel along?"

A Marked Man

Ambrose Bierce, one of several famous journalists and writers to see action, remembered most vividly the bizarre ironies of the war:

Among [the dead we left in the Cheat Mountain country in western Virginia, September 11-17, 1861] was a chap belonging to my company named Abbott; it is not odd that I recollect it, for there was something unusual in the manner of Abbott's taking off. He was lying flat upon his stomach and was killed by being struck in the side by a nearly spent cannonshot that came rolling in among us. The shot remained in him until removed. It was a solid round-shot, evidently cast in some private foundry, whose proprietor, setting the laws of thrift above those of ballistics, had put his "imprint" upon it: it bore, in slightly sunken letters, the name "Abbott."

THE WAR AT HOME

President Jefferson Davis

On February 8, 1862, delegates from seven Southern states set up a new nation—the Confederate States of America—and elected Jefferson Davis of Mississippi President. Constance Harrison, present at the inauguration, recalls the event:

The inauguration of Mr. Davis as President of the "Permanent Government" of the Confederate States . . . we viewed, by courtesy of Mr. John R. Thompson, the State Librarian, from one of the windows of the Capitol, where, while waiting for the exercises to begin, we read *Harper's Weekly* and other Northern papers, the latest by underground express. That 22nd of February, 1862, was a day of pouring rain, and the concourse of umbrellas in the square beneath us had the effect of an immense mushroom-bed. As the bishop and the President-elect came upon the stand, there was an almost painful hush in the crowd. All seemed to feel the gravity of the trust our chosen leader was assuming. When he kissed the Book a shout went up; but there was no elation visible as

'The gravity of the trust. . . .'   *33*

the people slowly dispersed. And it was thought omi-
nous afterwards, when the story was repeated, that,
as Mrs. Davis, who had a Virginian Negro for coachman, was driven to the inauguration, she observed
the carriage went at a snail's pace and was escorted
by four Negro men in black clothes, wearing white
cotton gloves and walking solemnly, two on either
side of the equipage; she asked the coachman what
such a spectacle could mean, and was answered,
"Well, ma'am, you tole me to arrange everything as
it should be; and this is the way we do in Richmon'
at funerals and such-like." Mrs. Davis promptly
ordered the outwalkers away, and with them de-
parted all the pomp and circumstance the occasion
admitted of.

» The Government Should Cease «

*In his Inaugural Address, President Davis refers to
the original Declaration of Independence to justify
secession and the creation of the Confederate States:*
Our present political position has been achieved in a
manner unprecedented in the history of nations. It
illustrates the American idea that governments rest
on the consent of the governed, and that it is the right
of the people to alter or abolish them at will when-
ever they become destructive of the ends for which
they were established. The declared purpose of the
compact of the Union from which we have with-
drawn was to "establish justice, insure domestic tran-

quility, provide for the common defense, promote the general welfare, and secure the blessings of liberty to ourselves and our posterity"; and when, in the judgment of the sovereign States composing this Confederacy, it has been perverted from the purposes for which it was ordained, and ceased to answer the ends for which it was established, a peaceful appeal to the ballot-box declared that, so far as they are concerned, the Government created by that compact should cease to exist. In this they merely asserted the right which the Declaration of Independence of July 4, 1776, defined to be "inalienable." Of the time and occasion of its exercise they as sovereigns were the final judges, each for itself. The impartial and enlightened verdict of mankind will vindicate the rectitude of our conduct; and He who knows the hearts of men will judge of the sincerity with which we have labored to preserve the Government of our fathers in its spirit. . . .

Food for the Troops

The great poet Walt Whitman worked with the wounded in Washington, D.C., throughout the war. He describes the helping hands at home:

The defeated [Union] troops commenced pouring into Washington over the Long Bridge at daylight on Monday, 22nd—a day drizzling all through with rain.

During the forenoon Washington gets all over

motley with these soldiers—queer-looking objects—strange eyes and faces, drenched (the steady rain drizzles all day) and fearfully worn, hungry, haggard, blistered in the feet.

Good people (but not over-many of them either) hurry up something for their grub. They put wash-kettles on the fire for soup, for coffee. They set tables on the sidewalks, wagonloads of bread are purchased, swiftly cut in stout chunks. Here are two aged ladies, beautiful, the first in the city for culture and charm —they stand with store of eating and drink at an improvised table of rough plank, and give food and have the store replenished from their house every half-hour all that day; and there in the rain they stand, active, silent, white-haired, and give food, though the tears stream down their cheeks almost without intermission the whole time.

Lee, Winning, Proposes Peace

Early in the war the Confederate fortunes looked bright. General Lee writes to President Davis in September, 1862:

The present posture of affairs, in my opinion, places it in the power of the Government of the Confederate States to propose with propriety to that of the United States the recognition of our independence.

For more than a year both sections of the country have been devastated by hostilities which have brought sorrow and suffering upon thousands of homes, without advancing the objects which our enemies proposed to themselves in beginning the contest.

Such a proposition coming from us at this time, could in no way be regarded as suing for peace, but being made when it is in our power to inflict injury upon our adversary, would show conclusively to the world that our sole object is the establishment of our independence, and the attainment of an honorable peace. The rejection of this offer would prove to the country that the responsibility of the continuance of the war does not rest upon us, but that the party in power in the United States elect to prosecute it for purposes of their own. The proposal of peace would enable the people of the United States to determine at their coming elections whether they will support those who favor a prolongation of the war, or those who wish to bring it to a termination, which can but be productive of good to both parties without affecting the honor of either.

Lincoln Consoles a Mother

The President wrote a Mrs. Bixby, of Boston, on November 21, 1864, comforting her on the loss of her sons in battle. No record of Mrs. Bixby's existence has ever been discovered, but the letter itself is justly famed for its eloquence:

Dear Madam,

I have been shown in the files of the War Department a statement of the Adjutant General of Massachusetts that you are the mother of five sons who have died gloriously on the field of battle. I feel how weak and fruitless must be any word of mine which should attempt to beguile you from the grief of a loss so overwhelming. But I cannot refrain from tendering you the consolation that may be found in the thanks of the republic they died to save. I pray that our Heavenly Father may assuage the anguish of your bereavement, and leave you only the cherished memory of the loved and lost, and the solemn pride that must be yours to have had so costly a sacrifice upon the altar of freedom.

Yours very sincerely and respectfully,

Abraham Lincoln

Resisting the Draft

In July, 1863, the Union adopted a compulsory draft —with the provision that a man could hire a substitute for himself for $300. Mrs. Charles Daly, wife of a prominent judge in New York City, kept a diary which contains the following account:

July 14, 1863

The draft began on Saturday, the twelfth, very foolishly ordered by the government, who supposed that these Union victories would make the people willing to submit. By giving them Sunday to think it over, by Monday morning there were large crowds assembled to resist the draft. All day yesterday there were dreadful scenes enacted in the city. The police were successfully opposed; many were killed, many houses were gutted and burned; the colored asylum was burned and all the furniture was carried off by women; Negroes were hung in the streets! All last night the fire-bells rang, but at last, in God's mercy, the rain came down in torrents and scattered the crowds, giving the city authorities time to organize. . . . I did not wonder at the spirit in which the poor resented the three-hundred-dollar clause.

» One More Victory «

The women of the South waited confidently for that one more victory which never came. Here, in an excerpt from Gone With the Wind, *one of the most famous novels ever written, Margaret Mitchell imagines their emotions:*

They loved their men, they believed in their men, they trusted them to the last breaths of their bodies. How could disaster ever come to women such as they when their stalwart gray line stood between them and the Yankees? Had there ever been such men as these since the first dawn of the world, so heroic, so reckless, so gallant, so tender? How could anything but overwhelming victory come to a Cause as just and right as theirs? A Cause they loved as much as they loved their men, a Cause they served with their hands and their hearts, a Cause they talked about, thought about, dreamed about—a Cause to which

they would sacrifice these men if need be, and bear their loss as proudly as the men bore their battle flags.

It was high tide of devotion and pride in their hearts, high tide of the Confederacy, for final victory was at hand. . . . How could it be otherwise with such leaders as Lee and Jackson? One more victory and the Yankees would be on their knees yelling for peace and the men would be riding home and there would be kissing and laughter. One more victory and the war was over!

Of course, there were empty chairs and babies who would never see their fathers' faces and unmarked graves by lonely Virginia creeks and in the still mountains of Tennessee, but was that too great a price to pay for such a Cause? Silks for the ladies and tea and sugar were hard to get, but that was something to joke about. Besides, the dashing blockade runners were bringing in these very things under the Yankees' disgruntled noses, and that made the possession of them many times more thrilling. . . .

So the women swished their silks and laughed and, looking on their men with hearts bursting with pride, they knew that love snatched in the face of danger and death was doubly sweet for the strange excitement that went with it.

Sackcloth and Ashes

In contrast to the swishing silks of Gone With the Wind *is this account of hardship from the diary of*

Emma LeConte, a 17-year-old Southern girl:

April 1st, 1865: Since my last entry on the 18th many events of importance have transpired. About ten days ago Father returned from Augusta bringing provisions, cloth, leather and tallow to make some candles—thus far we have had nothing but pine fire-light after dark. The provisions were flour, corn and bacon—a few hams, but chiefly the sides. I am so sick of bacon, it seems impossible for me to eat it. It seems as if I ought to when Father and the rest can eat it and think it good, but indeed my stomach turns against it and I usually make my dinner of hominy, corn bread and butter. The cloth is six bolts of factory cloth (unbleached homespun) which Father got at the very low price of only three dollars a yard. It makes me groan in spirit to think of wearing this heavy stuff as under-clothing all the hot summer. But, as Aunt Jane sagely observes, "it is better than nothing." Indeed, Cousin Ada and I agreed we would willingly wear sackcloth and even ashes if necessary, rather than give up to the Yankees.

MAN OF THE PEOPLE

» Forever Free «

*In September, 1862, President Abraham Lincoln di-
rected to the Confederacy an ultimatum, the* Emancipation Proclamation: *rejoin the Union, or forever
lose your slaves. He signed the* Proclamation *on New
Year's Day, 1863. It freed slaves only in the states
actively fighting the North; all slaves were not set
free until the passage of the 13th Amendment to the
Constitution. The* Proclamation *begins:*

On the first day of January, in the year of our Lord
one thousand eight hundred and sixty-three, all persons held as slaves within any State or designated
part of a State, the people whereof shall then be in
rebellion against the United States, shall be then,
thenceforward, and forever, free; and the Executive
government of the United States, including the military and naval authority thereof, will recognize and
maintain the freedom of such persons, and will do no
act or acts to repress such persons, or any of them in
any efforts they may make for their actual freedom.

» Lincoln, Man of the People «

Edwin Markham's moving poem, excerpted here,
contributed to Lincoln's legend:
Up from log cabin to the Capitol,
One fire was on his spirit, one resolve—
To send the keen ax to the root of wrong,
Clearing a free way for the feet of God,
The eyes of conscience testing every stroke,
To make his deed the measure of a man.
He built the rail-pile as he built the State,
Pouring his splendid strength through every blow:
The grip that swung the ax in Illinois
Was on the pen that set a people free.

» The Will of God Prevails «

In a melancholy mood in the early days of the war,
Lincoln puzzled over its religious meaning. His Med-
itation on the Divine Will *was not intended for pub-*
lication. He wrote it to clarify his own thinking:
The will of God prevails. In great contests each party
claims to act in accordance with the will of God. Both
may be, and one *must* be, wrong. God cannot be *for*,
and *against* the same thing at the same time. In the
present civil war it is quite possible that God's purpose is something different from the purpose of
either party—and yet the human instrumentalities,
working just as they do, are of the best adaptation to
effect His purpose. I am almost ready to say this is
probably true—that God wills this contest, and wills

'A clear way for the feet of God. . . .'   *45* that it shall not end yet. By his mere quiet power, on the minds of the now contestants, He could have either saved or destroyed the Union without a human contest. Yet the contest began. And having begun He could give the final victory to either side any day. Yet the contest proceeds.

» Brief and Pithy Remarks «

Out of the war and its causes came one of the most eloquent statements of all time—The Gettysburg Address. *Carl Sandburg sets the scene for Lincoln's immortal words:*

A printed invitation came to Lincoln's hands notifying him that on Thursday, November 19, 1863, exercises would be held for the dedication of a National Soldiers' Cemetery at Gettysburg. The same circular invitation had been mailed to Senators, Congressmen, the governors of Northern states, members of the cabinet, by the commission of Pennsylvanians who had organized a corporation through which Maine, New Hampshire, Vermont, Massachusetts, Rhode Island, Maryland, Connecticut, New York, New Jersey, Pennsylvania, Delaware, West Virginia, Ohio, Indiana, Illinois, Michigan, Wisconsin, and Minnesota were to share the cost of a decent burying ground for the dust and bones of the Union and Confederate dead.

In the helpless onrush of the war, it was known, too many of the fallen had lain as neglected cadavers rotting in the open fields or thrust into so shallow a resting place that a common farm plow caught in their bones. Now by order of Governor Curtin of Pennsylvania, seventeen acres had been purchased on Cemetery Hill, where the Union center stood its colors on the second and third of July, and plots of soil had been allotted each state for its graves.

Fifteen thousand, some said 30,000 or 50,000 people were on Cemetery Hill for the exercises . . . when the procession from Gettysburg arrived afoot and horseback representing the United States Government, the army and navy, governors of states, mayors of cities, a regiment of troops, hospital corps, telegraph-company representatives, Knights Templar, Masonic Fraternity, Odd Fellows, and other benevolent associations, the press, fire departments, citizens of Pennsylvania and other states. They were scheduled to start at ten o'clock, and at that hour on the clock Lincoln in a black suit, high silk hat, and white gloves came out of the Wills residence and mounted a horse. A crowd was on hand and he held a reception on horseback. At eleven the parade began to move. The President's horse seemed small for him, as some looked at it. Clark E. Carr, just behind the President, believed he noticed that the President sat erect and looked majestic to begin with and then got to thinking so that his body leaned forward, his arms hung limp, and his head bent far down.

Ward Hill Lamon introduced the President of the

United States. He rose, and holding in one hand the two sheets of paper at which he occasionally glanced, he delivered the address in his high-pitched and clear-carrying voice. The Cincinnati *Commercial* reporter wrote: "The President rises slowly, draws from his pocket a paper, and, when commotion subsides, in a sharp, unmusical treble voice, reads the brief and pithy remarks." Hay wrote in his diary: "The President, in a firm, free way, with more grace than is his wont, said his half-dozen words of consecration."

» The Gettysburg Address «

Fourscore and seven years ago, our fathers brought forth upon this continent a new nation, conceived in liberty and dedicated to the proposition that all men are created equal.

Now we are engaged in a great civil war, testing whether that nation—or any nation, so conceived and so dedicated—can long endure. We are met on a great battlefield of that war. We are met to dedicate a portion of it as the final resting place of those who have given their lives that that nation might live. It is altogether fitting and proper that we should do this.

But, in a larger sense, we cannot dedicate, we cannot consecrate, we cannot hallow, this ground. The brave men, living and dead, who struggled here, have consecrated it, far above our power to add or to detract. The world will little note nor long remember what we say here; but it can never forget what they did here. It is for us, the living, rather, to be dedicated here to the unfinished work that they have thus far so nobly carried on. It is rather for us to be here dedicated to the great task remaining before us; that from these honored dead we take increased devotion to that cause for which they have given the last full measure of devotion; that we here highly resolve that these dead shall not have died in vain; that the nation shall, under God, have a new birth of freedom, and that government of the people, by the people, for the people, shall not perish from the earth.

» An Inestimable Jewel «

Speaking to the 166th Ohio Regiment as it was being discharged on August 22, 1864, after long service, Lincoln emphasizes the basic reason for the war:

I suppose you are going home to see your families and friends. For the service you have done in this great struggle in which we are engaged I present you sincere thanks for myself and the country. I almost always feel inclined, when I happen to say anything to soldiers, to impress upon them in a few brief remarks the importance of success in this contest. It is not merely for today, but for all time to come that we should perpetuate for our children's children this great and free government, which we have enjoyed all our lives. I beg you to remember this, not merely for my sake, but for yours. I happen temporarily to occupy this big White House. I am a living witness that any one of your children may look to come here as my father's child has. It is in order that each of you may have through this free government which we have enjoyed, an open field and a fair chance for your industry, enterprise and intelligence; that you may all have equal privileges in the race of life, with all its desirable human aspirations. It is for this the struggle should be maintained, that we may not lose our birthright. . . . The nation is worth fighting for, to secure such an inestimable jewel.

» A Just, and a Lasting Peace «

The war neared its end, and the President looked beyond victory in his celebrated Second Inaugural Address, *delivered March 4, 1865. Its moving conclusion:*

With malice toward none; with charity for all; with firmness in the right, as God gives us to see the right, let us strive on to finish the work we are in; to bind up the nation's wounds; to care for him who shall have borne the battle, and for his widow, and his orphan—to do all which may achieve and cherish a just, and a lasting peace, among ourselves, and with all nations.

TO APPOMATTOX

» Each Dusty Road «

The war dragged on through the fall of 1864 and into the winter of 1865. These mournful lines from Stephen Vincent Benét's John Brown's Body *foretell the end:*

Army of Northern Virginia, haggard
    and tattered,
Tramping back on the pikes,
    through the dust-white summer,
With your wounds still fresh,
    your burden of prisoners,
Your burden of sick and wounded,
"One long groan of human anguish
    six miles long."
You reach the swollen Potomac at long last,
A foe behind, a risen river in front. . . .
So you splash and slip through
    the water and come at last
Safe, to the Southern side,
    while Meade does not strike;
Safe to take other roads,
    safe to march upon roads you know
For two long years.
    And yet—each road that you take,
Each dusty road leads to Appomattox now.

On April 2, 1865, under heavy Union pressure, Jefferson Davis and his cabinet fled the Confederate capitol at Richmond. But he was far from ready to give up, as these words from the proclamation he then issued indicate:

Animated by that confidence in your spirit and fortitude which never yet failed me, I announce to you, fellow countrymen, that it is my purpose to maintain your cause with my whole heart and soul; that I will never consent to abandon to the enemy one foot of the soil of any of the States of the Confederacy; that Virginia—noble State, whose ancient renown has been eclipsed by her still more glorious recent history; whose bosom has been bared to receive the main shock of this war; whose sons and daughters have exhibited heroism so sublime as to render her illustrious in all time to come—that Virginia, with the help of the people and by the blessing of Providence, shall be held and defended, and no peace ever be made with the infamous invaders of her territory. . . .

Surrender at Appomattox

On April 9, 1865, General Ulysses S. Grant met General Lee at Appomattox Court House to arrange the terms of Southern surrender. Grant's Memoirs recreate the somber dignity and cordiality of that occasion:

General Lee was dressed in a full uniform which was

entirely new, and was wearing a sword of consider-
able value, very likely the sword which had been
presented by the State of Virginia; at all events, it
was an entirely different sword from the one that
would ordinarily be worn in the field. In my rough
traveling suit, the uniform of a private with the
straps of a lieutenant-general, I must have contrasted
very strangely with a man so handsomely dressed,
six feet high and of faultless form. But this was not a
matter that I thought of until afterwards.

We soon fell into a conversation about old army
times. He remarked that he remembered me very
well in the old army; and I told him that as a matter
of course I remembered him perfectly, but from the
difference in our rank and years (there being about
sixteen years' difference in our ages), I had thought
it very likely that I had not attracted his attention
sufficiently to be remembered by him after such a
long interval. Our conversation grew so pleasant that
I almost forgot the object of our meeting. After the
conversation had run on in this style for some time,
General Lee called my attention to the object of our
meeting, and said that he had asked for this interview for the purpose of getting from me the terms I
proposed to give his army. I said that I meant merely
that his army should lay down their arms, not to take
them up again during the continuance of the war un-
less duly and properly exchanged. He said that he
had so understood my letter. . . .

When news of the surrender first reached our lines our men commenced firing a salute of a hundred guns in honor of the victory. I at once sent word, however, to have it stopped. The Confederates were now our prisoners, and we did not want to exult over their downfall.

I determined to return to Washington at once, with a view to putting a stop to the purchase of supplies, and what I now deemed other useless outlay of money. Before leaving, however, I thought I would like to see General Lee again; so next morning I rode out beyond our lines toward his headquarters, preceded by a bugler and a staff-officer carrying a white flag.

Lee soon mounted his horse, seeing who it was, and met me. We had there between the lines, sitting on horseback, a very pleasant conversation of over half an hour. . . .

Duty Done

As General Lee left the courthouse he found his men lined up outside. It was a stark, tragic moment for the tired officers and soldiers who had fought so long and so hard. A newspaper correspondent reports the scene:

It is impossible to describe the anguish of the troops when it was known that the surrender of the army was inevitable. Of all their trials, this was the greatest and hardest to endure. There was no conscious-

ness of shame; each heart could boast with honest pride that its duty had been done to the end, and that still unsullied remained its honor. When, after his interview with General Grant, General Lee again appeared, a shout of welcome instinctively went up from the army. But instantly recollecting the sad occasion that brought him before them, their shouts sank into silence, every hat was raised, and the bronzed faces of thousands of grim warriors were bathed in tears. As he rode slowly along the lines, hundreds of his devoted veterans pressed around the noble chief, trying to take his hand, touch his person, or even lay their hands upon his horse, thus exhibiting for him their great affection. The General then with head bare, and tears flowing freely down his manly cheeks, bade adieu to the army.

Lee's Farewell to His Army

On April 10, General Lee issued a moving farewell to his officers and men:

After four years of arduous service, marked by unsurpassed courage and fortitude, the Army of Northern Virginia has been compelled to yield to overwhelming numbers and resources. I need not tell the survivors of so many hard-fought battles, who have remained steadfast to the last, that I have consented to this result from no distrust of them, but, feeling that valor and devotion could accomplish nothing that could compensate for the loss that would have

attended the continuation of the contest, I have determined to avoid the useless sacrifice of those whose
past services have endeared them to their countrymen.

By the terms of the agreement officers and men can
return to their homes, and remain there until exchanged. You will take with you the satisfaction that
proceeds from the consciousness of duty faithfully
performed; and I earnestly pray that a merciful God
will extend to you his blessing and protection.

With an increasing admiration of your constancy
and devotion to your country, and a grateful remem-
brance of your kind and generous consideration of
myself, I bid you an affectionate farewell.

Conquest of a Song

*In Washington, Lincoln hoped peace would not bring
further punishment to the South—but he would soon
be dead and a harsh Reconstruction would begin.
Myrta Lockett Avary, who was present, remembers
Lincoln's tactful understatement of victory:*

General Lee's surrender had been announced; Washington was ablaze with excitement. On April 10,
1864, delirious multitudes surged to the White
House, calling the President out for a speech. It was
a moment for easy betrayal into words that might
widen the breach between sections. He said in his
quaint way that he had no speech ready, and con-
cluded humorously: "I have always thought 'Dixie'

one of the best tunes I ever heard. I insisted yesterday that we had fairly captured it. I presented the
question to the Attorney-General and he gave his
opinion that it is our lawful prize. I ask the band to
give us a good turn upon it." In that little speech, he
claimed the South by right of conquest of a song—
and nothing more.

Our Heritage

*Historian Bruce Catton eloquently summarizes the
significance of the Civil War to Americans:*

We are people to whom the past is forever speaking.
We listen to it because we cannot help ourselves, for
the past speaks to us with many voices. Far out of
that dark nowhere which is the time before we were
born, men who were flesh of our flesh and bone of our
bone went through fire and storm to break a path to
the future. We are part of the future they died for;
they are part of the past that brought the future.
What they did—the lives they lived, the sacrifices
they made, the stories they told and the songs they
sang and, finally, the deaths they died—make up a
part of our own experience. We cannot cut ourselves
off from it. It is as real to us as something that happened last week. It is a basic part of our heritage as
Americans.

CHRONOLOGY

1860 Abraham Lincoln elected President.
South Carolina secedes from the Union.

1861 January-February, six Southern states secede.
February 18, Jefferson Davis inaugurated
as President, Confederate States of America.
April 12, attack on Fort Sumter, S.C.
April-May, four border states secede.
July 21, first battle of Bull Run (Manassas),Va.
September 1, Gen. Ulysses S. Grant assumes
Union command in Missouri.
September 21, Gen. Robert E. Lee, C.S.A.,
takes command of forces in Valley of the
Kanawha, Va.

1862 March 7, Battle of Pea Ridge, Ark.
March 9, Battle of *Monitor* vs. *Merrimack*.
April 6-7, Battle of Shiloh, Tenn.
April 26, Occupation of New Orleans, La.
September 17, Battle of Antietam
(Sharpsburg), Md.

September 22, Lincoln issues *Emancipation Proclamation*.

December 13, Battle of Fredericksburg, Va.

1863 January 1, Lincoln signs *Emancipation Proclamation*.

July 1-3, Battle of Gettysburg, Pa.

July 4, Vicksburg, Miss. surrendered.

November 19, Lincoln delivers *Gettysburg Address*.

November 24-25, Battles of Lookout Mountain and Missionary Ridge, Chattanooga, Tenn.

1864 May 5, Battle of the Wilderness (Virginia).

July 12, Gen. Jubal Early, C.S.A., attacks Washington, D.C.

July 22, Battle of Atlanta, Ga.

August 5, Battle of Mobile Bay, Ala.

December 15, Battle of Nashville, Tenn.

1865 February 17, Gen. William T. Sherman captures and burns Columbia, S.C.

March 4, Lincoln's second inauguration.

April 2, Battle of Selma, Ala.

April 9, Lee surrenders to Grant at Appomattox, Va.

April 14, Lincoln assassinated.

April 26, Gen. Joseph E. Johnston surrenders to Sherman at Durham, N.C.

May 26, Gen. Kirby Smith surrenders trans-Mississippi area to Gen. Edward Canby, ending organized resistance.

Set at The Castle Press in Intertype Walbaum, a light
open typeface designed by Justus Erich Walbaum (1768-1839),
who was a type founder at Weimar.
Printed on Hallmark Eggshell Book paper.
Designed by Harald Peter.